CONTENTS

Chapter 1: Up, Up, and Awaaaaay!   5

Chapter 2: The Famous Wright Flight   8

Chapter 3: Have a Safe Trip!   18

Chapter 4: Flying in the Future   36

But Wait . . . There's More!   42

FUN STUFF

How Airplanes Get from Here . . .
to There!

by Jordan D. Brown
illustrated by Mark Borgions

Ready-to-Read

Simon Spotlight
New York   London   Toronto   Sydney   New Delhi

SIMON SPOTLIGHT

An imprint of Simon & Schuster Children's Publishing Division

1230 Avenue of the Americas, New York, New York 10020

This Simon Spotlight edition May 2016

For information about special discounts for bulk purchases, please contact Simon & Schuster Special Sales at
1-866-506-1949 or business@simonandschuster.com.

The Simon & Schuster Speakers Bureau can bring authors to your live event. For more information or to book an
event contact the Simon & Schuster Speakers Bureau at 1-866-248-3049 or visit our website at
www.simonspeakers.com.

Manufactured in the United States of America 0416 LAK

2 4 6 8 10 9 7 5 3 1

Cataloging-in-Publication Data for this title is available from the Library of Congress.

ISBN 978-1-4814-6164-1 (pbk)

ISBN 978-1-4814-6165-8 (hc)

ISBN 978-1-4814-6166-5 (eBook)

Chapter 1
Up, Up, and Awaaaaay!

Your heart is pounding, and your palms are sweaty. The pilot just announced that your plane will take off any minute. You check that your seat belt is tightened, and then look out the window. The plane's engines roar as the aircraft races down the runway. Faster and faster, and then—you're in the air! Soon the houses and cars below look like tiny toys.

You wonder about the amazing flying machine you're on. How does a heavy airplane fly in the air? How does the pilot steer? And why are your ears clogged? By the end of this book, you'll know the answers to these questions and more, and be a Science of Fun Stuff Expert on the exciting world of airplanes!

Every day millions of people fly on airplanes. Most passengers are more concerned about snacks and crying babies than they are about being so high up. Long ago, things were different. No one thought we could fly as high as birds. Then the Wright brothers changed everything. They used science and stick-to-itiveness to invent the first successful airplane.

Chapter 2
The Famous Wright Flight

If you ask people, "Who invented the airplane?", most will say, "Easy. The Wright brothers!'" Some might even know that the brothers' first flight took place in Kitty Hawk, North Carolina, in 1903. But if you ask people to tell you *how* Orville and Wilbur Wright created the first powered airplane, they'll probably say, "Hmmm . . . I'll get back to you."

Many people don't know that before the Wright brothers succeeded, they faced many obstacles and disasters. Critics told them they were wasting their time, and to give up. But the Wright brothers ignored the critics. They kept asking questions, did *years* of careful experiments, and always learned from their failures. In short, they acted like scientists.

Their first successful flight happened on December 17, 1903. On a windy day, on a beach in North Carolina, Orville flew their plane for twelve seconds and traveled 120 feet. Then, later that day, Wilbur piloted their plane for fifty-nine seconds and flew more than 850 feet. Success! After many years of hard work, they had finally done it! But what were the steps that led to that day?

Flash back to the 1890s: Orville and Wilbur owned a bicycle shop in Dayton, Ohio. The brothers loved designing and repairing bikes, but they were also very curious about human flight. People had already flown in hot-air balloons and gliders, but these aircraft had many accidents because they were tricky to control. The brothers believed they could do better.

So they did some research. They read as many books as they could on the science of flight. They wrote letters to scientists and inventors, asking lots of questions. They studied birds to see how the birds' wings helped the animals steer and glide. In 1901, in order to test different wings' strength, they built a machine called a wind tunnel. It used a strong fan to blow air.

The Wright brothers flew gliders (aircraft without engines) in 1900, 1901, and 1902. But although their 1903 plane had an engine, it didn't have the same innovations as a modern plane, so they needed to figure

out many aspects of how to control it, such as a way to control the plane's roll (how the wingtips tilt up and down).

Wilbur discovered a great solution by accident. One day in the bike shop, he was twisting a long cardboard box back and forth while chatting with a customer. Aha! He realized that they could twist the plane's wings the same way using ropes, to help them steer.

When they had enough information, they built unpowered gliders—for more than two *years*! For safety, they flew these planes on ropes, like a kite. To test them out they took a train about six hundred miles to Kitty Hawk, North Carolina. They chose that place because the winds there are constant.

And they knew they needed lots of wind to get their gliders off the ground. Orville and Wilbur tested more than two hundred different wings and made more than a thousand flights on gliders. A tool called an *anemometer* helped them measure wind speed. They used math to figure out how to build and improve the parts. By experimenting, they became better pilots too.

After they mastered the glider, they added a motor to help the plane take off and stay in the air. They first considered a car engine, but it was too heavy. So the brothers built a lighter motor themselves. They even made their own propellers.

After their first successful flight in Kitty Hawk in 1903, the Wright brothers kept experimenting. They wanted a plane that could stay in the air for *hours,* not minutes, and could safely land. By 1905 their plane (called the Flyer III) could stay in the air a long time and even fly in circles. Their hard work had paid off, which was good news for them and for the inventors who followed and improved on their early efforts. And great news for everyone who loves to fly today!

Chapter 3
Have a Safe Trip!

Today even before you board a plane, science is part of the airport experience. At security the guards ask everyone to walk through a metal detector. They want to make sure that no one is carrying anything dangerous, such as a weapon or an explosive. If the machine goes *Beep! Beep! Beep!* it means that a person could be carrying a weapon—or that the person simply forgot to remove their belt, which has a metal buckle.

So how does this machine "know" if something is made of metal? The secret is *electromagnetism*. Scientists used to think that electricity and magnetism were different, but in the 1870s, James Clerk Maxwell discovered that they are parts of the same thing. In both electricity and magnetism, invisible particles called *electrons* flow from one atom to another to create a magnetic field.

When you walk through the detector, you pass next to a coil of wire called a *transmitter* coil. Electricity flows through this coil, creating a magnetic field around it. If you have any metal on you, the magnetic field detects it and sends a signal to a loudspeaker that beeps.

A Peek Inside Your Bags

As you walk through the metal detector, your carry-on bags move through a machine that uses X-rays, which are a type of high-energy light that we cannot see.

You may have seen X-ray pictures in the dentist's or doctor's office. These pictures can show what your teeth and bones look like under your skin.

X-rays can travel through soft materials other than the skin too, such as plastic and leather, but not as well through metal. That's why X-rays are great for searching for metal weapons.

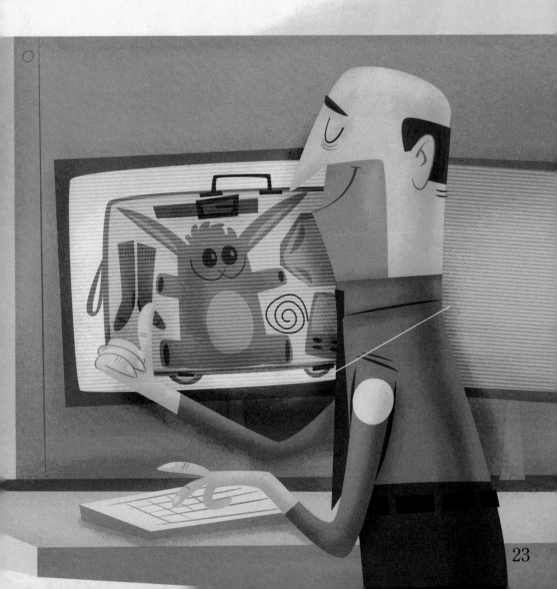

A Nose for Security

Airport security experts sometimes get
help from dogs. These dogs are specially
trained to sniff out materials used to make
explosives. As you probably know, dogs have
an amazing sense of smell. You have about
five million scent receptors in your nose.
Sounds impressive until you realize that some
dogs, such as bloodhounds, have about *three
hundred million* receptors in their noses!

Training bomb-sniffing dogs takes a lot of time. Over and over, special trainers hold the smell of an explosive near a dog's nose. After training a dog to learn what explosives smell like, if the dog sniffs and recognizes it anywhere outside the training area, the dog gets a treat, such as a toy or a snack. To train and care for a bomb-sniffing dog can cost more than two hundred thousand dollars a year! But the animals are very good at what they do and are an important part of keeping airports safe.

Why Birds and Planes Fly— But You Can't

Have you ever wished you could fly like a superhero? You know, leap into the air and speed through the clouds? Sadly, no matter how hard we flap our arms, we're not going anywhere. The reason that we can't fly—but birds and planes can—is *physics*. Physics is the science of matter, motion, and energy.

According to physics, there are four forces that affect a plane: weight, drag, lift, and thrust.

Weight is a downward force caused by the Earth's *gravity*. Gravity is an invisible force that pulls objects together. Bigger objects have more gravity than smaller things. Earth is *much* bigger than a ball, so when you toss a ball up, it is pulled down. A jet plane is a very large object that gravity pulls down on.

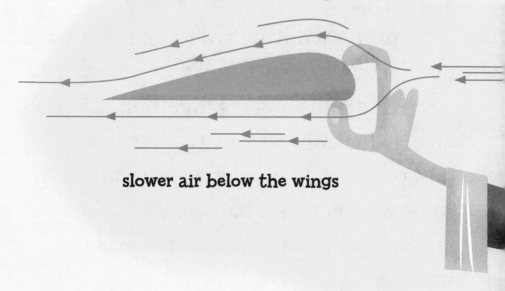

faster air above the wings

slower air below the wings

A second force, *drag*, is the force that pushes against an object that is moving forward. Air seems to be made of nothing, but it's actually made of tiny gas molecules. Even though you can't see them, you push through a sea of molecules every day when you're running to class, or rounding second base on the baseball field. When a plane flies through the sky, drag tries to slow it down.

A third force called *lift* pulls planes upward. When a plane moves quickly through the air, the curved shape of its wings forces the air *above* the wings to move faster than the air *below* the wings. The slower-moving air under the wings gives the plane a push upward. The idea of lift was explained by a Swiss scientist named Daniel Bernoulli.

And finally, the fourth force called *thrust* pushes planes in the direction of motion. Engines produce thrust. For a plane to fly up, the upward force (lift) must be greater than the downward force (weight), and the forward force (thrust) must be greater than the backward force (drag).

Think about it like this—planes fly by going up and forward, right? So lift (up) and thrust (forward) have to be strongest.

Because of physics, a paper airplane can fly, but the kid who threw it can't. (Without a jetpack, of course!)

How a Pilot Steers

After an airplane takes off, passengers watch a movie, read a book, or take a nap.

Not the pilot! He or she has the job of making sure the plane flies safely. Planes move in three directions known as *pitch*, *yaw*, and *roll*. "Pitch" relates to the nose of the plane going up and down, "yaw" describes turning left or right, and "roll" refers to how the wingtips tilt up and down.

To control pitch, the pilot raises or lowers the *elevators*. These are horizontal flaps on the plane's tail. When the elevators are lowered, the plane's nose dives; when they are raised, the plane climbs. To change the yaw, the pilot steps on pedals that control the *rudder*, a vertical flap on the tail of the plane. The rudder turns the plane left or right. Finally, to change the plane's roll, the pilot turns a wheel called the *yoke* that raises or lowers the *ailerons*, which are flaps on the wings.

Things That Go Bump in the Sky

The pilot sometimes tells passengers to return to their seats and buckle up because of *turbulence*. This means that air currents could be rough and shake the plane. Don't worry, though. Pilots are trained to handle these disturbances, and planes are made to stand up to tough turbulence.

Feeling nervous? Keep this in mind: bad turbulence is *very* rare. If a ride starts to get bumpy, put on your seat belt and try to distract yourself.

Stuffy Ears

When a plane takes off or lands, your ears may feel clogged or painful. What's up? Normally the pressure inside and outside your eardrum is balanced. But when a plane takes off or lands, there's a *sudden* change in air pressure. The pressure is different on each side of your eardrum. Chewing gum or yawning can make your ears "pop" because these actions open a tube in each ear. This relieves the pressure.

Chapter 4
Flying in the Future

Imagine if the Wright brothers could ride on an airplane today. They'd be thrilled, shocked, and amazed. Air travel has changed in *so* many ways since their time. For example, jets have become bigger, faster, and way more powerful. What will airplanes look like in fifty years? Or a hundred? Scientists love to dream up wild new ideas to solve problems.

One wild idea is windowless airplanes. Windows might not seem like a problem, but they weigh a lot all together. If there were no windows, the plane would be lighter and need less fuel. Less fuel could save money and cause less pollution. Of course, passengers still want to see outside. So some scientists propose that *all* the inside walls of the plane be covered with video screens, which are lighter than windows.

These screens would be hooked up to computers and cameras. The cameras would take a video of everything that was going on outside the plane. This "improvement" might make flying on an airplane scarier for some people!

It's a Bird! It's a Plane! It's Both. Scientists at NASA (the National Aeronautics and Space Administration) sometimes look to nature for ideas when they design new aircraft. One example is the Solar Flapper. While it doesn't exist yet, this airplane would be powered by the sun, and its wings would flap like a bird's. Another energy source that scientists are considering for planes is body heat. They're not saying that body heat would power the whole plane, of course, but it would be used to make simple gadgets work.

SCIENCE
OF FUN STUFF
EXPERT
on
AIRPLANES

- -

Congratulations! You've reached the end of this book and are ready for landing. You are now an official Science of Fun Stuff Expert on airplanes. So the next time you board an airplane, remember the physics behind the fun.

Hey, kids! Now that you're an expert on the science of airplanes, turn the page to learn even more about the Wright brothers, air travel today, and how to make a paper airplane!

The Wright Brothers
"If birds can glide for long periods of time, then . . . why can't I?" —Orville Wright

Orville and Wilbur Wright grew up in Dayton, Ohio. Wilbur was four years older than Orville. The boys were both creative and inventive and were always fascinated by anything that flew. When the two boys were small, their father brought them a toy helicopter. It was an inexpensive gift, and the boys thought it would probably fall to the ground after a second or two. They were thrilled and shocked when it flew clear across the room! Orville and Wilbur were inspired to make their own toy helicopters. Years later as an adult, Orville said it was the toy helicopter that had strengthened the two brothers' interest in flight.

As adults Orville and Wilbur worked together in several different businesses, and in 1892 they created the Wright Cycle Company and sold bicycles. Although the business was doing well, they were bored and wanted to do something more creative with their spare time. Their interest in flight was sparked again in 1896 when they heard about Otto Lilienthal, a famous glider experimenter, and Samuel Langley, who had successfully launched an unmanned Aerodrome. The Wright brothers decided to create a flight machine that was powered by an engine and heavier than air.

The Wright brothers conducted many experiments in the back room of their bicycle shop.

Once the brothers felt they were ready to test their gliders and eventually their airplane, they needed the perfect spot. They wrote to the United States Weather Bureau for help. They were told that Kitty Hawk, North Carolina, would be a good testing area because it had constant winds and sand dunes. (In case of a crash landing, the ground would be soft.) The Wright Brothers tested unpowered gliders at Kitty Hawk in 1900, 1901, and 1902 before they felt they were ready to test their plane.

The big day finally arrived on December 17, 1903. Orville and Wilbur brought their plane to Kitty Hawk, North Carolina. It was decided that Orville would man the controls, while Wilbur pushed the plane down a short wooden ramp, and it lifted into the air.

Many people did not believe that the Wright brothers invented a machine that could carry people and fly. So the brothers began doing flight demonstrations to show off their invention. Finally, in 1908, President Roosevelt contacted the brothers and they agreed to a deal to build an airplane for the US Army. Orville and Wilbur continued to design planes until Wilbur's death in 1912.

43

Air Travel by the Number

The Wright brothers' first flight was only twelve seconds long and a distance of 120 feet. Now check out the distances on these modern-day flights. Orville and Wilbur would be amazed (and proud!) at how far their invention has come!

Some of the World's Longest Nonstop Flights

Toronto to Hong Kong: 7,810 miles and 15.5 hours

This is the longest commercial flight out of Canada. It treats passengers to breathtaking views of Victoria Harbour in Hong Kong as they land.

New York to Johannesburg: 7,969 miles and 16 hours

This flight from John F. Kennedy airport in New York to Johannesburg has been around for a long time. This particular flight has been running for more than forty years! It's apparent that people think a chance to visit one of South Africa's largest cities is worth the trip.

Dallas to Sydney: 8,578 miles and 17 hours

Stretch out your legs on this flight from Texas to Australia. With seventeen hours to kill, you'll have enough time to read up on koalas and kangaroos to be considered an expert by the time you land!

Some of the Biggest Commercial Airplanes

Airbus A340-600
420 passengers

The Airbus A340-600 is a passenger airplane from France that can hold more than 400 passengers. Its maximum cruising speed is 580 miles per hour.

Boeing 747-8
700 passengers

The Boeing 747-8 is a passenger airplane manufactured in the United States. It can hold an impressive 700 passengers and can reach a maximum cruising speed of 649 miles per hour.

Airbus A380-900
850 passengers

The Airbus A380-900 is a passenger plane from France. It is currently the biggest passenger airplane in the world! It can hold a staggering 850 passengers and can reach a maximum cruising speed of 676 miles per hour.

Make a Paper Airplane!

(Use an 8 ½ x 11 piece of paper.)

1. First fold the paper in half, hot-dog style. ("Hot-dog style" means to fold the paper lengthwise to make a vertical line, so the paper is long and narrow like a hot dog.)

2. Unfold the paper.

3. Fold the top two corners into the center line. Fold the top diagonal edges to the center.

4. Fold the entire plane in half along the first, hot-dog-style fold.

5. Fold one wing down so that the short unfolded part of the wing is flush with the bottom edge of the plane's body.

6. Repeat step 5 with the other wing.

7. Unfold the last two folds so that the wings are perpendicular to the body of the plane.

8. Fly your paper airplane!

Tip: When you fly your paper plane, make sure that the airplane is level with the ground.

47

Being an expert on something means you can get an awesome score on a quiz on that subject! Take this

SCIENCE OF AIRPLANES QUIZ

to see how much you've learned.

1. Air is made of

   a. nothing   b. dust   c. gas molecules

2. What pulls planes upward?

   a. lift   b. thrust   c. drag

3. What does pitch mean, in terms of airplanes?

   a. when a plane turns left and right   b. when the wingtips tilt up and down   c. when the nose of the plane moves up and down

4. When your ears "pop" on an airplane, that means

   a. you ate too many snacks   b. there was a sudden change in air pressure   c. there was a lot of turbulence

5. Physics is the science of matter, motion, and

   a. energy   b. music   c. art

6. To learn about flight, the Wright Brothers studied

   a. butterflies   b. birds   c. turtles

7. Where did the very first air flight take place?

   a. Dayton, Ohio   b. Brooklyn, New York   c. Kitty Hawk, North Carolina

8. What machine did the Wright brothers build to test the lift and drag of different airplane wings?

   a. propellers   b. an anemometer   c. a wind tunnel

Answers: 1. c 2. a 3. c 4. b 5. a 6. b 7. c 8. c